T0067898

PEACE WITHIN THE STORM

When Life Hurts and God Heals

ALEXANDRA STONE

WESTBOW
P R E S S®
A DIVISION OF THOMAS NELSON
& ZONDERVAN

Pencil Portraits by Dana
www.portraitsbydana.com
http://www.facebook.com/portraitsbydana

WestBow Press books may be ordered through booksellers or by contacting:

WestBow Press
A Division of Thomas Nelson & Zondervan
1663 Liberty Drive
Bloomington, IN 47403
www.westbowpress.com
1 (866) 928-1240

ISBN: 978-1-5127-8527-2 (sc)
ISBN: 978-1-5127-8529-6 (hc)
ISBN: 978-1-5127-8528-9 (e)

Library of Congress Control Number: 2017906224

Print information available on the last page.

WestBow Press rev. date: 04/27/2017

For God, my Heavenly Father who urged me to tell my story. For Lucas and Lilly-Grace, I love you as far as the East is from the West.

Contents

Preface: Tied up in Ribbons and Bows................................ ix

Chapter 1 1

Chapter 2... 11

Chapter 3... 17

Chapter 4... 21

Chapter 5... 33

Chapter 6... 45

Chapter 7... 57

Chapter 8... 63

Chapter 9... 69

Chapter 10 75

Chapter 11 81

Chapter 12 87

Chapter 13 91

Chapter 14 97

Epilogue: Letter to Ainsley Pearl................................105

PREFACE: TIED UP IN RIBBONS AND BOWS

Why is it that we, as women, do this to ourselves? We cover things up, sweep things under the rug, and hide things behind closed doors so that our lives are tied up in pretty bows with pretty boxes wrapped in pretty wrapping paper.

Untie the bow, and rip the paper off. Inside is the dark stuff, the stuff we have hidden so that no one on the outside could ever know. We live with the secrets and we live with the regrets of the decisions we have made in weak moments. Women shame themselves and each other so much more than men could ever possibly comprehend. I believe that we are afraid. We fear judgment of others, and mostly of other women. That is why when we were really upset all night with grief, anxiety, or depression, we "fake it until we make it" when we go outside of our homes with a plastered smile and nice makeup. And when people ask us, "How are you?" in casual conversation, we reply, "I'm fine. How are you?" And the cycle continues.

I ask you, "How are you, really?"

I am not always fine, and I don't want to pretend that I am. Sometimes I just want to say, "This day is not my best. I want to go home and cry. I need to let it all go for three seconds while I loathe in self-pity."

If I said that in the small town I live in—*whew*! News would be traveling so fast that I had lost it, and who knows what other rumors would begin? It would make your head spin. That is why we wrap up pretty bows and stuff our boxes full of the hidden shame. This can't be healthy. It creates blocks of emotion, and those walls that we build are terrible for our health, our mental state, and our Christian walk.

The Lord doesn't want the bows, He doesn't want the pretty wrapping paper; what He wants is what's in the box, ugly and all. He doesn't say, "Give me the good." He says, "Give me your *all*." This means the good and the bad—even the *really* bad. When I was grieving the loss of Ainsley Pearl, I felt major anxiety and could not even admit to myself the feelings were okay. I felt shame in all its nasty glory surrounding me and pulling me in, saying, "Tie it up, and make yourself look good, wash your tears off, and get that makeup back on."

It's a lie.

God calls us to be honest with Him, honest with our Christian brothers and sisters, and honest about our faith.

The truth is Christianity is not easy, and it doesn't make life simpler, I believe it makes it tougher. Because the devil is our enemy, our competitor, and one of shame's closest friends. The devil wants our defeat because we are the Lord's. He wants to create problems for us, and he will supply all the most beautiful bows you could ever imagine. The Lord wants open, raw, and real.

If we never give *Him* the real, we are not trusting *Him* fully and relying on *Him* 100 percent. We somehow think by making it hidden that we can make it all okay and have some hold of control in the situation. It took me over a year to admit to myself, let alone anyone else, that I faced depression. I was so ashamed and utterly embarrassed to say that I, as a Christian, was depressed.

I have had people tell me—and have even heard preachers teach—that people who take medicine for this type of thing are not true or real Christians. The worst thing is that I believed them. I thought that if I could not control my emotions and grief on my own with the help of the Lord, that I was not a true Christian.

This is such a lie.

I fought this battle within myself for over a year and a half before I ever began to take medicine. It was horribly difficult for me to ask someone for help in this way. I just knew that my struggle to control my mind and emotions was a failure on my part, and that is just how I felt. This in turn fueled my feelings of depression.

I will never forget when I went into my family doctor's office. I explained that I had lost a daughter and was struggling with some anxiety over trying to cope. The holidays were coming up and I thought I might need help, if she thought it might be okay for me to take something. She was absolutely willing to help me out, but I was so embarrassed about the whole ordeal that I would not even go into the pharmacy for fear of someone in the town finding out.

As if it wasn't enough for her to tell me it was okay and I was, in fact, normal, I sought the opinion of my OB. I told him how I was struggling with the day-to-day and felt overly protective of Lilly Grace. I was having almost a sense of paranoia over her protection. I could not sleep without having dreams about her being taken or worse. The dreams would wake me every time I slept, so I didn't want to fall asleep at all. They were so terrible I could not even mention them out loud, but they haunted my mind. I cherished and loved this child with every ounce of my being, and the thought of someone hurting her literally tore my heart to shreds. I cannot imagine how the Lord felt seeing his Son on the cross.

At times, I had flashbacks of the hospital rooms I was in. I can remember daydreaming and vividly seeing myself lying in the hospital bed with a scalpel over my throat before the tracheotomy. When I had these visions or flashbacks, it wasn't like it was the first time when I felt peace; it was a distorted image of panic and fear. I felt as if Satan were trying to steal this serene time I had with the Lord away from me.

I tried to verbalize as best I could to my husband, but even he couldn't understand what I was going through. I felt that I had lost my purpose in life and didn't know where I belonged anymore. Most of all, I felt ashamed for feeling this way.

My OB determined that I had posttraumatic stress disorder. When I was telling him of my symptoms, he replied that he had been expecting me to come in sooner and wasn't at all surprised to see me.

I began to feel like myself again. It was a wonderful choice for everyone around me as well as for me. I became the wife I always had been, the Christian I used to be, and the person I knew I really was. I am such a happier person and better Christian because of it. I was able to talk and be open about my struggles. At first, I only admitted to having anxiety, which I did, but there was more than that. It took me so long to admit to others that I faced depression. Once I realized that there is no shame in that, I felt so much freedom to tell other women. When I first began to share, I was almost hesitantly waiting for the floor to fall out beneath me and for someone to laugh in my face. That's not what happened though; they were accepting and, in turn, opened up to me.

Once I started sharing, I found the number of women who have faced similar situations to be astounding! Once I was willing, it was as if the Lord just opened up a new avenue in my life. I was able to share with so many women and was shocked to know the shame that they too faced with the "secret" of depression. If you are reading this and have ever felt depression or still do today, know it's okay and that you're not a bad person, parent, wife, sibling, daughter, or Christian. The Lord does not fault you, and He doesn't expect you to be perfect. He wants the best you have to give him. And for me, this is how it began.

Shame can be a funny thing……..

Growing up, shame was a powerful figure in my life. That may sound strange, but as I look back, I can see it so clearly. I was a perfectionist, a pure perfectionist in everything. In school, in sports, in plays, in church, and in my family, I wanted everything to be just right all of the time. I held myself to such a high standard that was really unrealistic, but as I thought at nine years old, I could be the one to break through to be in the number one position at everything. This need to be the best stemmed from my desire to get attention from those around me.

I desired positive attention and praise from my parents. I tried so hard throughout my entire youth to be the best. I created major stomach problems for myself at a very young age, worrying about being at the top. This was a bow thing too. My mother did so much to protect us from the evils of the world and she, not knowing, was wonderful at tying up ribbons and bows. In my life, things were not accepted well if they were not "acceptable." In many towns, a lot of this had to do with the image in the community and how things needed to be presentable.

When my sister got pregnant in high school, it was hard to process those feelings. She chose to give that sweet baby life and raise him at sixteen years old. She could have very well chosen to abort, like many girls do now, but she didn't. She stayed up at night when he had colic, changed his diapers, fed him every four hours, and loved him with her whole heart.

Some people in the family were covered up in shame over this. Even in big towns, it turns out that people talk and shame is bold. It takes a nasty form, even when we don't intend for it to.

When my sister decided to have this child, it was tough on all of us, but she did what she needed to do and chose the more difficult path.

I caused myself stomach ulcers trying to make my box of life look like a blue-ribbon winner. It was so important to me to be perfect that I lost the fun of childhood. The devil and his buddy shame took that away from me. Stealing is one of his favorite games, but that was only the first thing he took from me.

In high school, the need to be perfect continued. At soccer, I had to be the best player, the fastest and most aggressive. In cheerleading, I had to be captain. In academics, I had to be in the top rankings. In beauty pageants, I had to be the winner. I craved the top of everything, thinking that would give me love. In my eyes, love was somewhat conditional.

As a child, seeing unprocessed emotions within the family around me created much anxiety for me, knowing that if I messed up or disappointed them in some way, I would also receive the treatment she had. I know that they didn't intend for it to be this way, but from my perspective as a child, it seemed true.

So I pushed on, and I struggled on the inside, but all the while, I was adding more ribbons and bows to my ever-growing box of the hidden fear, shame, and embarrassment.

No matter how much I fought to be the best, the empty hole never became full; it was never enough. I was still lacking and always felt the void.

Six months before my wedding, I gave in to the Lord Jesus Christ. The void was gone, the need to be perfect was gone, the shame was gone, and the guilt was erased. I had found the Lord and became his child the minute I asked him into my heart and became a saved daughter. The Lord rescued me. Even though my husband was wonderful and genuine, I still needed something to fill that empty hole inside and to throw away my pretty box. He did that for me. He took it and accepted me, flaws and all. This was the happiest moment of my life, and I cried uncontrollably, letting go of everything in complete surrender to Him. That was the ultimate love, the unconditional kind—the kind that wasn't ashamed of what was inside my box. Praise the Lord!

I was with a group of ladies this week and we spent two hours talking about shame. It was eye-opening to me how this nasty little thing can become so large in our lives. As I spoke with them, they all shared stories of shame and how it stole joy from their lives. Shame was present in their lives so strongly it convinced them that they should hide things. I hid my ugliness, and so many women around the world do this too.

The Lord doesn't ask us to hide. He asks us to bring our cares to him, even the ugly ones. He asks us to be a light. How can we be a light to those around us if we all are shoving our boxes full and putting ribbons on top to make them look nice? How can we be a light if we are hiding in the dark? We won't be the kind of light the Lord wants; we will be a dimly lit corner in the room.

Don't deal with the burdens of the past on your own.

It is too much.

No matter the issues we face as women, or just as humans in general, we shouldn't face them alone, and the Lord didn't intend for it to be that way. We shouldn't feel embarrassed when things don't go how we planned. We should feel the pain and the emotions that go along with it and work through them, no matter how difficult it may be. When we trick the world into believing that we have perfect lives, we only impress ourselves. The more we turn the focus to things of the world, the more like this world we become: fake, unrealistic, unreal, and cold.

Have you ever noticed that light doesn't represent cold but signifies warmth? And no matter how much we mimic the original light with bulbs and flames, there is no warmth like that of the Son. When we bask in the Son's light, we are covered in genuine warmth, like that of a loving father's embrace.

Chapter 1

Many people find it hard to share their faith or to testify; I used to be one of those people. I let fear get in my way. I let doubt cloud my mind and suffocate my urge to tell what God had done in my life. I no longer let the devil's whispers in my ear direct my decisions or alter my choices. I have learned to fully lean on the Lord and follow His path only. This is when the serenity that comes with confidence overtook me. I have never felt so stable in my decisions in my life as when I am doing what the Lord asks me to do. It has taken me years to get there, and this is where it began.

From my experiences, I have learned to live without regrets, to tie up loose strings, and to not let the worry that comes with lost words conquer me. Sharing the gospel—or the lack of doing so—used to be a regret and a big fear of mine. I felt the Holy Spirit urging me to tell my story. I came up with so many reasons not to for four years. I felt that people might think I was dumb, that they may not believe me, or that I wasn't wise enough in my knowledge of the Bible. I hadn't memorized scripture or taught Bible studies, I hadn't been in church my whole life, and I couldn't recount all the characters in the Bible. My fear was completely wrapped up in what people thought about me or what they might think, including the shame that could follow me for messing up, fumbling over my words, or making mistakes. There was something missing from my thoughts about sharing my testimony—something that made all the difference in the world. The thing I missed was that the Holy Spirit was not urging me to share for my glory but for His own. The Lord wanted me to share so that seeds would be planted and the great harvester could reap.

It's my time now to obey.

> For man does not see
>
> what the Lord sees, for
>
> man sees what is visible,
>
> but the Lord sees the heart.
>
> —1 Samuel 16:7

I was in church some as a child; I attended Sunday school, ate cookies, and drank fruit punch. It was fun, but I can't say that I got anything out of it, other than the social skills that any little one gets at that age. It wasn't until my twenties that I realized how important Sunday school really was. This was where the real training began, and this is where I missed out.

After early elementary school, we stopped going to Sunday school but still made it for regular church services. I attended youth group on Sunday nights though, and that's where I realized I was about to come of age. This was not like coming of age in *Frozen,* where parties are thrown and magic happens; this was the age of accountability.

At the age of thirteen, I was in a class for three months. This was the supposed "age of accountability." I learned that this age is different for many people and that there is no class required to obtain salvation. There, we learned about the founder of the church and what it meant to be baptized.

For the graduation of the class, we went to the Elk River in Tennessee and got dunked in waist-deep rushing water. All of my friends and family came to support me in this act of submission, and I can remember being so proud of myself. I knew they were proud that I was a Christian, and to their knowledge, I really was. This just goes to prove that no one knows your heart but you and the Lord. As they all stood on the nearby sandbar watching me walk out to the water, I felt nothing but pride in myself for making them proud of their daughter.

I can still recall the emptiness of that moment.

Prior to the cold water washing over my head, I repeated the prayer for salvation directly after the preacher, who was holding my body from swishing away in that river. The problem was that I repeated the words but felt nothing.

Jesus wasn't present in that act or in my heart. I hadn't invited him, and he hadn't convicted me. It was a pretense.

By definition, the word *pretense* means an attempt to make something that is not the case appear true; it is a claim, especially a false or ambitious one.

Well, this act was an attempt, false, and ambitious. I didn't do it for attention; I did it because I thought it was the right thing to do. I had the purest motives. I didn't understand that it took more to become saved. I honestly didn't know. And they didn't either.

What my family and friends didn't know was that all I did that day was repeat after a preacher and get a chilly bath. I had made them proud though, and that made me happy—for the time being.

> Some never get started on their destiny
> because they cannot humble themselves
> enough to grow, learn, and change.
> —Author unknown

Through junior high and high school, I claimed to be a Christian and honestly thought I was one. I think this was based on appearance. When I think about growing up in those times, I realize that my supposed Christianity was a front for being a "good girl." This was also a way to make my parents and other adults in my life proud of me.

I was a pleaser from as far back as I can remember, and I still am today; the only difference is that the aim dramatically changed.

In my youth, I tried to please my parents, my friends, my advisors, and my teachers. I had a great deal of anxiety when I was growing up and face it sometimes still. I developed stomach issues from the stress that I placed on myself. In the fourth grade, I was diagnosed with gastritis, IBS, and acid reflux. My stomach hurt all of the time, and I stayed very nauseated as a result.

My parents divorced when I was three years old, and I think that over the years that situation caused me to try to please everyone and be a fixer. I wanted them all to get along and love each other, as well as my sister and me. My mother remarried, and my stepfather was always present in my life financially and physically but not emotionally. I never doubted that he would take care of our needs and help us to get most things we wanted, but he never became that fatherly figure I craved. I visited my dad every other weekend and every other week in the summer. We had a great relationship, but I thrived on him being proud of me. I always wanted to impress him and to be the apple of his eye.

Maybe I thought that the more I did to impress him, the prouder of me he would be—and somehow that was attached to love. The image of a family wasn't what I saw in my life. And that deeply troubled me. It was difficult for me to digest all of this, and I yearned to make it "normal."

It got to the point where I didn't want to go out of the house, and if I was out past ten o'clock at night, I would throw up. It did not matter where I was or who I was with, if it was past ten and I saw the clock, it was over.

My dad loved to take us to do fun things. We were constantly going to concerts, hockey games, vacations, and more. I always had a great time, but my need for security in my family outweighed the need for fun. I became a top student in my class, became the best I could be athletically, and was a shining star everywhere. Most of my glowing childhood looked absolutely amazing from the outside looking in, but the little girl in my mind needed something more. I wanted to be a doctor, travel to New York, and change the world, but all of those massive ambitions were just a result of that growing need to make people proud of me.

I suffered from anxiety and even went to counseling in middle school. In high school, my little brother was born to my dad and stepmom, and I can remember being unsure of my emotions. When they told me, I cried. I tried to be so happy for them, and I knew that was what they had desired for a long time, but I could not help my emotional pain and confusion. It wasn't until I was saved that I realized the only one that I have to please is my godly Father, and that love is unconditional.

Now my only aim is God. I have realized that God's happiness with me is what matters, and if I mess up or fail, which happens often, He will not be upset with me or disappointed in any way, shape, form, or fashion. We don't have to earn His love— not that I had to earn the love of my parents, but being a perfectionist, I felt I had to.

God's love can't be earned. He does appreciate our efforts and works, but they won't gain us access to Him in heaven. That is only earned through salvation. Once that is obtained, the Lord will be there endlessly, never loving us differently because of what we did or didn't do.

CHAPTER 2

I began dating the man who is now my husband and attending church with him in a small Baptist church in the country. I began to ask my husband questions about salvation and the assurance of heaven. I asked him often,

> How do I know I am saved?
>
> How do I know I am a Christian?
>
> How do I *really* know if I am going to heaven?

I was under conviction for a year before I realized what that nagging feeling in the pit of my stomach was.

I will never forget January 30, 2010, which was only six months before my wedding, because the song "So Much to Thank Him For" was being sung as a special in the morning church service. I had heard this song three or four times, and while I loved the song, it never had affected me quite like this.

I began to cry and didn't stop until the end of the service. These, mind you, were not the cute sniffle tears but the big, ugly, makeup-smeared, red-nose, blubbering kind of tears. The woman sitting beside me thought I was crazy and that something was terribly wrong with me. She even asked if I was okay, and all I could muster was, "I got saved."

And sometimes while on this way,
I kneel, and I stop and say,
"Thank you for all you've
Done for me."

That gospel song just overwhelms me when I think of it! How could it not? I think we all can relate to the writer of this song at some point in our lives. We should feel this way every day, shouldn't we?

At nineteen, I was saved and became a Christian, a daughter of the Lord, Jesus Christ. I could not stop smiling and am smiling to this day thinking of the overwhelming joy I possessed in those moments. I have never felt that indescribable joy since, but I know that will come again when I meet my Lord in heaven face-to-face and take Him by the hand. I believe that everyone should experience that unmistakable and utter joy that comes with salvation.

It's a feeling like no other,
as if the weight of the world has been
lifted off your shoulders,
the emotional walls have been broken down,
and the floodgates have been opened.
It is as if there's not one single burden
weighing heavy on your mind
and nothing else matters
at that moment but the Lord

and your undeniable assurance

of His home in heaven.

This description can't even compare to the glory I felt in my heart that day. Magnificence, splendor, beauty, wonder, grandeur, brilliance, or even exaltation can come close but not encapsulate the majesty of the moment salvation covered me.

Acts 2:37–41 gives a great description of Salvation. In these verses, Peter is speaking to the house of Israel, testifying of the Lord and urging them to become saved.

When they heard this, they were pricked in their
heart, and said unto Peter and to the rest of the
apostles Men and brethren what shall we do?
—Acts 2:37

I love the way the King James Version lays this out so simply. The word "pricked" is used. When someone gets his or her finger pricked, it hurts but it's not devastating or life threatening. But when you look closer, the term they annotate for "pricked" is "cut to the heart." That really gives a great visual! Pricked versus cut to the heart—you tell me which one gets your attention more! The people literally felt cut to the heart with conviction and looked to him for an answer.

I was baptized later in the month at the same church as an outward expression to show my salvation.

Then Peter said unto them, repent, and be baptized every one of you in the name of Jesus Christ for the remission of sins, and ye shall receive the gift of the Holy Ghost.

—Acts 2:38

It's that easy, and it was that day for me too! I also felt cut to the heart and needed a solution. The only resolution was through Jesus.

And with many other words did he testify and exhort, saying, Save yourselves from this untoward generation.

—Acts 2:39

So on that day, my fiancé and soon-to-be in-laws came up to the front of the church with me and stood. I felt like it was a right of passage that I was determined to complete. I was so nervous to stand in front of the church, but I knew I had to do it.

I believe that God knew I would need Him through the coming years—and for the rest of my life. He knew the pain and trials that were coming. He knew storms would roll in. I thank Him for saving me before the storm struck and shattered my world.

Chapter 3

My husband and I began to discuss the prospect of having a baby and expanding our family.

My mother had many difficulties with pregnancy and unsuccessful conception, so I feared that it would be a long road ahead for me as well. My husband and I thought it would be several years before we could have a child, but again, the Lord makes the plans—not us! We took the proper steps and conceived on the *first attempt* in August 2012.

The at-home pregnancy-test companies could make a fortune off of me. I was so paranoid and always had the notion in my head that I needed to take one, just in case, so I usually had a stockpile in my bathroom cabinet at home under the sink. I had taken about five at-home tests since we had started trying, and they were all negative. It had only been a week, and the label on the box says, five days earlier. Really it was too soon, but I kept convincing myself, "You never know."

Finally, one morning at 5:00, I woke up and ran to the bathroom because I just had a feeling I was pregnant. Mother's intuition, I guess.

When those two lines appeared, I could have shouted with joy! My mind was spinning with excitement. I just couldn't believe it.

Lucas was still in the bed asleep and I wanted to be really cute and clever and figure out some way to surprise him, so I withheld my secret for the time being. This was so impossible that I almost blurted out the news one hundred times. We do not keep things from each other—*ever*—so this was really quite impossible. I went to get a blood test that day, and it was confirmed!

I was so excited I couldn't stand it! I called my OB/GYN and made an appointment right away.

I was at a yard sale later that morning with three of my friends, and I just couldn't stand it. I blurted it out, and they all squealed in delight. We concocted many reveal ideas, but in the end, I couldn't keep a secret from him, no matter what it was. We were attending a birthday party, and right before going in, while sitting in the paved driveway, I said, "Guess what. I have something I need to tell you." And he responded, "You're pregnant."

The first few weeks became problematic rapidly, a lot more than I anticipated. I found myself nauseated all night and all day, every single day. I called out of work so often that I ended up taking leave because I couldn't even take three steps, let alone walk, without getting very sick.

I had to have a bucket or toilet with me at all times!

The smell of food …

The thought of food …

The taste of food …

Ugh. It was too much!

Even crackers were gross to me! The only thing I tolerated was orange juice, so I drank a ton of it. And I liked milk. I never had many cravings, other than milk. I would drink two gallons a week of whole milk. For some reason, I wanted it thick. That sounds so revolting now, but then, I considered it the thicker the better. I craved the consistency of buttermilk. Ugh!

The remainder of August, I stayed in bed, only getting up for necessary trips to the restroom. My doctor called this normal morning sickness in the beginning, but I knew in my gut it was something more. I was given antinausea medicine by the OB to help with the sickness, but it was just getting worse and worse by the hour.

CHAPTER 4

I tested so many tricks to help with nausea, but again, nothing. I tried pressure bands, vitamin B suckers, antisickness cream, antisickness pills, crackers before sitting up, ice chips, antinausea suppositories, ginger root, and I was still sick.

Nothing was working.

By this point, I had lost fifteen pounds in one month. My husband and I went to the appointment with my OB, and they conducted my first ultrasound. My husband was with me, sitting by my left side, and the ultrasound tech was to my right. I was doing some serious deep breathing to try to not get sick on the table, but the excitement I had to see the baby outweighed my need to expel my stomach contents right there on that ultrasound machine.

She showed us our baby, our little dot of life, and we were all aglow, smiling from ear to ear. I had tears in my eyes at the first glimpse of this sweet baby that was really ours. Then, as the tech was wrapping up her measurements and wiping goop off my belly, she exclaimed, "Oh, wait!"

I immediately thought something was wrong with our little one and quickly became very panicky. All I could think about was my mother's history and how I could possibly have believed that I could be successful in childbearing so soon. I just knew history would repeat itself and I would be facing what she had so many times.

The tech then said, "I think I see something down here," and she moved around to get a better reading with the wand and more goop. She then replied, "Congratulations. You have twins."

I think my mouth literally hit the floor. I started to cry and looked at my husband. He was also smiling, but

I honestly think we were both in shock. I don't know if it was fear or excitement, or both, but it was something emotional and life changing! She looked confused and told us to wait one moment while she got someone more experienced. When they returned, the head tech looked without explanation and then got out a textbook. This gave me a great deal of confidence—*not.*

They were in one sack, making them identical twins, but they were lacking a membrane wall. She then told us to not get too attached because often one will not make it and ultimately disappears.

Already, at this moment, I became a mother hen who was protective of *both* of my little chicks. I didn't even listen to her because I knew that wouldn't happen. I had two babies; they were mine.

I would later learn they were the Lord's first and mine and Lucas's second.

After seeing the doctor that day, we left the office, only to come back a couple of days later. I can remember sitting in the driveway on the phone with my mother-in-law and was just crying and crying and asking her to pray for both of my babies because I didn't want anything to happen to either one of them. This strong Christian woman assured me she had been, she would, and that everything would be okay. The fear began to encompass me at that moment and the tech's words came back haunting my mind. It felt like they weren't even giving my babies a fighting chance.

I had no idea how my faith and marriage vows were about to be dramatically tested.

My brethren, count it all joy
when ye fall into various trials: knowing this, that
they testing of your faith produces patience.
—James 1:2

I was admitted to the hospital two times over the next weeks for IV fluids, due to extreme sickness and dehydration. My doctor concluded that I had hyperemesis, which is a fancy term for just being very sick. The twins also made me sicker because double the baby, double the hormones, double the sickness.

My days over this month consisted of being in the bed all day, every day. I was so sick that I could literally not walk to the bathroom, five feet away, without getting sick. I lay in the bed as long as possible without getting up until the last minute. We didn't even have satellite! I had five channels and books, but reading made me sick too. I was always very tired and slept for eighteen hours a day. I was under constant supervision, for I was unable to be left alone. I would not let anyone bring food into the house, and even my husband had to eat outside. I am so very thankful for my friends and family who stayed with me during this time. They rotated out and helped me do basically everything. I had no strength to walk or stand, no energy to move, was completely exhausted, and was burning up every minute of the day. I know I wasn't pleasant to be around.

The fall was quickly approaching, with it my birthday and my favorite season of the year. This year, though, was unusually cold. My heat strokes came more and more often, and I felt like I was literally in a furnace all of the time. I had my husband leave all of the windows open constantly, and I lay in the bed in tank tops and shorts with two fans pointed on me, even during thirty-degree nights.

Lucas, a great man, slept in layers of clothing and sweat suits under piles of blankets trying to keep warm, but he let me do my thing and didn't complain about it. I laugh thinking of that image in my mind, but at the time, I didn't think it was too funny.

I had a lot of time to think and reflect on my growing family and thanked the Lord daily for my twins. I imagined my home with twins and planned our nursery room. I researched car seats and double strollers, matching onesies, and family pictures. I felt so special to be given the gift of these children. These were the first twins in our family on either side, and I knew it wasn't a mere accident like the nurses and doctors had claimed. I can remember when we were on our way home from the ultrasound and Lucas and I called our parents to tell them the good news. I called my mom, a teacher, and said, "Are you sitting down or can you get somewhere away from the class?" She was in the lunch line. She asked another teacher to watch her class and stepped to the side. I announced, "I am having twins," and I heard her shouting with glee through the phone speaker. *"Really?"* she said. I assured her it was the truth, and she was overwhelmed. She was telling her teacher friends with me still on the phone.

My husband called his father and mother, and they had similar reactions. They just couldn't believe it. Everyone was immediately wrapped up in my pregnancy right along with me, caring for those babies with all of our hearts.

In this time of complete bed rest, I also begged God a lot. You see, I was terrified, living in a state of fear that something would go wrong. I am naturally a happy and bubbly person, and I tried so desperately to hang on to any shred of that when I was pregnant, but the fear and desperation began to creep in at times. Looking back, I can see moments of depression. That was difficult for me to admit to myself, because I felt if people knew how I really felt inside, they would be disappointed in me and ashamed.

I began to memorize Psalm 23. Every time those dark thoughts would come upon me, I would recite this scripture without hesitation.

The Lord is my shepherd; I shall not want.

He maketh me to lie down in green pastures;

He leadeth me beside the still waters.

He restoreth my soul;

He leadeth me in the paths of righteousness

For His name's sake.

Yea, Though I walk through the

Valley of the shadow of death, I

Will fear no evil:

For thou art with me;

Thy rod and thy staff

They comfort me.

Thou prepare a table before me

In the presence of mine enemies:

Thou annoinest my head with oil;

Peace within the Storm

My cup runneth over.

Surely goodness and mercy

Shall follow me all the days of my life:

And I will dwell in the house of the Lord

Forever.

Instead of having beautiful hair, my hair was falling out in huge clumps. I stopped brushing it at times because so much would be in the sink; I feared I would go bald. I could run my fingers through my hair and come back with a handful. I remember looking at myself in the mirror after showering one day, and as I stood there with the help of Lucas, I thought, *Who is this person?* I looked so frail. I could see my ribs protruding, to the point they could be counted, and my backbone was poking out all the way down my spine. Underneath my big belly, my hipbones distended. I did not feel like the beautiful pregnant woman I had dreamed of being, that many women claim to feel like. In this state, I could barely walk or stand. My husband showered me and washed my hair. He even shaved my legs! What an awesome man and a blessing. He was so unbelievably strong for me. I never thought of what that might have looked like to him.

One night when I was feeling particularly depressed, he carried me in his arms to my in-laws' house, across the driveway, and set me in their huge tile shower. He let me lie there and rest in the water for what seemed like an hour. It was so soothing and very helpful for my body and soul. He helped me get dressed daily. With the exception of doctor's appointments, I never even saw the kitchen or living room in my house for weeks at a time. He kept up everything with the help of family, cared for me, and worked a full-time job as a farmer in the middle of harvest season, the busiest time of the year. Every night when he got home and every morning before he left, he kissed me and told me how much he loved me. He never even complained to me about any of it. I don't know what I would've done without him.

Even though it was so terrible, I believe this is where I needed to be for the Lord to lift me up and for me to rely fully on him, rather than on myself.

And he said unto his disciples; therefore I say unto you, Take no thought for your life, what ye shall eat; neither for the body, what ye shall put on.

The life is more than meat and the body is more than raiment. Consider the ravens: for they neither sow nor reap; which neither have storehouse nor barn; and God feedeth them: how much more are ye better than the fowls?

And which of you with taking thought can add to his stature one cubit?

If ye then be not able to do that thing which is least, why take ye thought for the rest?

Consider the lilies how they grow: they toil not, they spin not; and yet I say unto you, that Solomon is all his glory was not arrayed like one of these.

If then God so clothe the grass, which is to day in the field, and to morrow is cast into the oven; how much more will he clothe you, O ye of little faith?

And seek not what ye shall eat, or what ye shall drink, neither be ye of doubtful mind.

For all these things do the nations of the world seek after: and your Father knoweth that ye have need of these things.

But rather seek ye the kingdom of God; and all these things shall be added unto you.

Fear not, little flock; for it is your Father's good pleasure to give you the kingdom. Sell that ye have, and give alms; provide yourself bags which wax not old, a treasure in the heavens that faileth not, where no thief approacheth, neither moth corrupteth.

For where your treasure is, there will your heart be also.

(Luke 13:22–34)

CHAPTER 5

As tradition went, my mother cooked chili at her house for Halloween. I had already spent my birthday in my sickbed and really wanted to get out of the house. My husband carried me to my mom's, a good twenty minutes away, and we enjoyed the night together. I didn't eat chili, of course, because I couldn't eat anything more than crackers and orange juice!

That year, the fall season was unusually cold, requiring jackets and toboggans in October, but I was *hot!*

As the night was coming to an end, we headed home, and I began to feel violently ill. I was trying so hard to get home without getting sick, and I made it to the end of our road before jumping out of the truck and landing on the ground and heaving for five minutes straight. The neighbor's dog even came to visit me!

That was the night before my life changed forever.

I know if I had just been sick like normal mothers during my pregnancy, I would not be where I am today. If I had not had the next day go as it did, I would not have the relationship I have with Jesus as so many yearn to possess. I am thankful, humbled, and a servant. I became a servant the day I was saved, but these next moments were what taught me to hang on to God and to never let go.

I was admitted to the hospital in Huntsville, Alabama, a third time the next day for more IV fluids. I was already taking Zofran and Phenergan every four and six hours for the sickness, but it did no good. At this point, I was less than one hundred pounds, having lost twenty-three pounds—while pregnant with twins in my second trimester. I stayed for a few days, receiving medicine in my IV and more fluids. My OB decided to run an extra test on my thyroid, just to be sure, and he would send the labs to a referring endocrinologist if anything was abnormal.

The morning I was to be sent home, I began to feel somewhat odd. My husband had already left for work, and my aunt was coming to visit around 10:00 that morning. My nurse, straight out of nursing school, was not on my normal rotation. (You see by this point, I had made friends with all of my nurses.) I told her I wasn't feeling well and felt like my heart was racing a bit. She checked my pulse, and it was above the normal range. She called for the OB, and he sent for the cardiologist. My heart rate continued to incline, and I was sent to get an EKG at the main hospital.

A tech was called to transport me, and we wheeled off. We made it to the EKG room, where there was a line. With bucket in hand, I informed the tech I was going to get sick and that he might want to look away. The EKG tech recognized that I was very ill and moved me to the front of the line. This was God's interference!

I received the EKG and all looked normal, other than my escalated heart rate. The babies also looked normal. I answered her questions, and we began our journey back to my hospital room.

As we arrived at the tram, I felt worse. My tongue was swelling and I knew my words were not correct. I began having trouble breathing as well, but my tech was not trained in medicine. I began to panic. I thought I was having a stroke. I just knew that when I looked in the mirror, half of my face would be drooped down and permanently scarred from this moment. I was attempting to get the attention of my transporter but failed miserably. I even saw a nurse on the way back walking in the main lobby, and I looked at her with pleading eyes and an aching heart. She looked back at me but kept moving. She couldn't help me; only God could get to me at this point.

Your most profound and intimate experiences of worship
will likely be in your darkest days—
when your heart is broken,
when you feel abandoned,

when you're out of options,

when the pain is great—

and you turn to God alone.

—Rick Warren

When we finally arrived to my room in what seemed like a four-hour trip down the hall, my nurse came back in to check my vitals. My aunt was in the room, God's interference again, and she was looking at me very strangely. I told the nurse I didn't feel right and something was wrong with me, and she acted as if I was normal! I was speaking to her like someone with major speech impediments and she didn't even seem concerned. My aunt, however, did!

I could hear my words

but it wasn't my voice.

It was wrong,

all wrong.

I know my aunt saw fear in my eyes, for I had never been this afraid before.

As the nurse left the room, my aunt ran into the hallway to the nurses' station and demanded something was wrong and to see the charge nurse.

Romans 8:26 says,

> Likewise the Spirit also helped our infirmaries:
> for we know not what we should pray for as we
> ought: but the Spirit itself maketh intercession for
> us with groanings which cannot be uttered.
> Even when I could not speak, the Holy Spirit
> interpreted on my behalf to the Lord.

The charge nurse comes into the room, along with the cardiologist who was still on the hall. They took my vitals and the cardiologist asked my aunt, "Does she always talk like this?" Of course she said no. My nurse hurriedly ran out of the room and called the OB on the hall. They both came into my room and saw my pulse was at 205 beats.

This meant my heart pumped faster than blood could go in; basically, my heart was pumping itself dry and empty.

I'm sure you know that an empty heart cannot sustain life. There is only one problem with science; *it doesn't factor in Jesus.* You see, my heart was not empty but full, so full that it was overflowing with the Holy Spirit, who lived in me.

He sustained my life not with my blood but his.

My flesh and my heart

may fail,

but God

is the strength

of my heart

and my portion

forever.

—Psalm 73:26

The OB doctor and the charge nurse, who was also pregnant at the time, unplugged my bed and literally hauled me to the ICU. It was a scene from a movie.

He yelled at her to get out of the way and grabbed my headboard; he dared someone to get in the way. He had, just minutes before, received my lab report from the thyroid screening and seen I was in the middle of a thyroid storm.

The clinical presentation includes fever, tachycardia, hypertension, and neurological and GI abnormalities. Hypertension may be followed by congestive heart failure that is associated with hypotension and shock. Because thyroid storm is usually fatal if left untreated, rapid diagnosis and aggressive treatment are critical.

Fortunately, this condition is extremely rare. When it speaks of the storms in the Bible and how Jesus calmed them with the wave of his hand, in my case, this was literal. Down the halls, I was in and out of consciousness and in a state of utter peace.

How could I be at peace, you ask, when I couldn't breathe or talk and my heart was pumping out of my chest, sucking the very life out of me? Well, that's a question for God.

The peace of God that passeth

all understanding

washed over me,

and I was ready to go to the Lord.

—Philippians 4:7

I watched the fluorescent lights above me as I moved and was the calmest I have ever been in my life.

Jeremiah Denton, admiral in the US army during the Vietnam War, was captured after his plane was shot down and he, along with the other POWs, was placed in a concentration camp for Vietnamese Prison for POWs. He was tortured for seven and a half years, but in that time, he found God. He states in his book, "I offered myself to God with an admission that I could take no more on my own. Tears ran down my face as I repeated my vow of surrender to him. Strangely, as soon as I made the vow, a deep feeling of peace settled into my tortured mind and pain-wracked body, and the suffering left me completely. It was the most profound and deeply inspiring moment of my life."

This is similar to what I experienced. Nothing nearly as traumatic as being in a POW camp by far, but facing death? I can relate. As the ICU nurse kept yelling at me to stay awake and to breathe, I couldn't. I could inhale, but the air was blocked to come back out. I choked out a couple of breaths, only by God's grace, and they took both of my arms and began to prod needles in them.

I was very frightened of needles, even after all of those IVs, and I despised them with all of my might. I was awake enough to know they were doing it, but it didn't hurt me at all. I was just calm and ready to go meet the Lord. I grabbed a nurse's hand as she was walking by and held on. She grabbed mine back, as if to say it was okay, but honestly they were all scared from the look in their eyes.

I said, "Hold my hand," not that anyone could understand me. But you know who did? Jesus. *He held my hand.*

Not in my mind but on the table. I didn't see him, but I knew—as much as I know my name is Alexandra—that he held my hand—my left hand—and didn't let go. He calmed the storm inside me and saved my life that day.

I feel that it is imperative to mention that Jesus held onto my left hand, rather than my right. It was not until I began writing my testimony that I realized the significance of this.

As I was lying down, He was to my left, with my left hand! If He was on my left, then that means that I was to his right and he was holding my left hand with his right hand. You see, this is amazing to me and confirms even more that this experience is God.

> Nevertheless, I am continually with the:
> thou hast holden me by my right hand.
> —Psalm 73:23

> My soul followeth hard after thee:
> thy right hand uphold me.
> —Psalm 63:8

> Even there shall thy hand lead me, and
> thy right hand shall uphold me.
> —Psalm 139:10

> Thou hast also given me the shield of thy
> salvation: and thy right hand hath holden me
> up, and thy gentleness has made me great.
> —Psalm 18:35

There are fifty-eight Bible verses speaking of Jesus's *right* hand. The power lies within that message, and if that's not God, then I don't know what is!

CHAPTER 6

Nurses were literally propelling pills down my throat, and I saw a large man standing at the foot of my bed. I heard him yell, "Run to the pharmacy. We only have five minutes!" He then said, "Get the trache ready." Just as the nurses were beginning to prep me for a tracheotomy, my throat opened, and I gasped for air.

The nurse ran back in with the medicine, shoved it down my throat, and then there was silence.

We waited. Well, they waited, and I was just lying there in my state of peace.

I slept and doctors, nurses, and my family came in a few at a time to visit me. I remember seeing my mother through the glass door crying and hugging the doctor over and over and then my husband coming up behind him. They looked terrified, but I still had no clue what had actually happened. In my mind, I had a stroke. That was about all the thought I could muster.

They both came in and were in shock. They hugged me and asked me how I was doing, but I don't really remember a lot about the next several hours.

My in-laws, aunt, grandparents, sister, dad, and stepmother came, but other than smiling and saying hello, I was pretty unaware of my circumstances. My doctor had instructed my family to keep me in the dark for trying to keep my heart rate under control.

I knew I had not had a stroke and my thyroid went berserk, but it wasn't until two weeks later that I begged my husband to tell me what happened. The thyroid storm began to shut my organs down and cause my heart to pump too fast. They gave me large doses of iodine to stop my thyroid all together, along with twenty thyroid pills daily. I was also on blood pressure medicine and two nausea medicines as well.

My husband told me that when he got there the doctor told him that he had done all he could do and we would just have to wait and see how my body reacted. It was all God's doing that the endocrinologist was even there that day, but he happened to be doing rounds in the ICU and was there before I even arrived. He canceled his patients for the day and did not leave my bedside for three hours until he was sure I was stable, or as stable as I could be. He also informed my family that throughout the entire storm, my blood pressure stayed within normal range. He had never in his career seen that happen. Thyroid storms only happen to 1 percent of the population, and in every case, the blood pressure causes the patient to have a stroke or go into a coma—with the exception of me. That's not scientifically logical. It's God again.

If the nurse had not made it to the pharmacy and back within five minutes, I would have died.

If the on-call OB had not been on the hall and rushed me to the ICU, I would have died.

If the charge nurse had not called the on-call OB, I would have died. If my aunt had not recognized I was in danger, I would have died.

The charge nurse and OB had, in fact, never even seen a thyroid storm and only recognized the symptoms from their college textbooks. If I had not gone first in the line at the EKG and waited for an extra fifteen minutes, I would have died.

You see, God was there.

He put every minute in to motion for a reason.

Every minute.

If any one minute would have played out differently,

I would not be here today to share my testimony.

Although I was hooked up to what seemed like one hundred cords and tubes, I was a happy camper. My babies were still alive, and Jesus had held my hand. How many people can say that Jesus touched them? He touched me—literally touched me.

Every time I hear the song "The Unseen Hand" by the Gaithers, I get emotional and think back to those days.

There is an unseen hand to me
That leads through ways I cannot see.

This hand has led through shadows drear
And while it leads, I have no fear.

When I finally got moved out of the ICU and to a regular room, a maternal fetal medicine doctor came to visit me, per my OBs request. He gave me an ultrasound and viewed my little ones in depth. He asked my husband and me if we knew their gender, and of course we did not, so he told us we were having identical twin girls.

This was so exciting, and I just basked in joy—for all of one minute. In the next minute, he informed us that they had a problem.

My girls had something called twin-to-twin transfusion syndrome. This is where the girls share blood vessels and are connected through the veins. They ultimately have the same blood that recycles through each other's body.

Then we were presented with the options.

We were given a day to make a choice.

Choice 1: Do nothing. The girls would go into heart failure, and my body would have a mirror effect and do whatever their bodies did. So when they went into heart failure, I would too.

Choice 2: End the pregnancy by forced labor.

Choice 3: Travel to have a surgery, that I might not even be a candidate for, and separate the blood vessels. If I had the surgery and one girl did not make it in time, the blood from her body would dump into the other's and cause a hemorrhage, which would cause severe brain damage, resulting in mental retardation.

How can a mother and a father choose this? The devil had literally backed us into a corner and applied force for us to choose. This, however, was not the devil's choice to make, and it wasn't ours either.

Christ is far above any ruler or authority or power
or leader or anything else, not only in the world
but also in in the world to come. He is the Supreme
One, not this stronghold, not the lies the stronghold
has been erected on, not the enemy who has
waged war against me. Christ is far above.

—Ephesians 1:21

Over the next day, we sought the counsel of our preacher and many other dear people in our lives. We wanted an answer. It wasn't so easy either. We both were taught and raised not to abort, and that was something we felt very strongly about.

My doctors, though, were very sure that my body would not withstand the pregnancy. This meant that if I continued, I would leave my husband without the girls and me. If I did nothing, I might get the girls farther along with a chance of them going to twenty-four weeks, the viable age outside the womb. Even then, they would be less than one pound and would likely not survive.

I can remember our preacher at the time visiting us, and I asked him, as well as everyone else who came that day, what he would do. What would he and the others choose? It wasn't fair for me to ask people that kind of question, but I so desperately craved an answer.

A clear answer.

I wanted God to just come down to my little hospital room, take my face in His hands, look me in the eye, and tell me, "Alex, this is what I want you to choose." It didn't work that way. I didn't feel any clear answers one way or the other, but I did know that I was not signing a piece of paper to take them away from me. That is something that I don't think I could have lived with for the rest of my life.

> Be still
>
> And know that
>
> I am God.
>
> —Psalm 46:10

This verse calms me and terrifies me at the same time. Being still is difficult for me. Utter stillness in the presence of the Lord is something that I have to work diligently on, and I am sure something I will work on forever. To me, this is one of the most powerful verses in the Bible, yet so small and simple. There are no complex words requiring footnotes, a dictionary, or a commentary. The largest word in this scripture is *still*, and it is only made up of five letters. *Still.* This verse and word signifies complete relinquish of absolute control. No holding on, not one silk thread attached. I tried to be still in this moment and allow the power of the Lord to seep into my hospital room. I couldn't feel him, and I couldn't make out a decision, a sign, or his voice. Ultimately, I gave up control and, though I was overcome by the tragic events of the past two weeks, gave it over.

Not my will, but yours be done

—Luke 22:42

When it came down to it, we said that we were not making a decision and the Lord had to make it for us. I was in a state of denial.

Later that day, my doctor came in and said, "We are sending you to Birmingham's children's hospital. Pack a bag; you will be coming home without the girls."

They had made the choice to terminate the pregnancy, and I had not. I was glad it was in the Lord's hands, but I couldn't believe this was the future for my precious babies.

I did not want this.

On the ride to Birmingham, I felt like someone outside my own body looking in. I was considerably calm for the circumstances but felt as if it weren't real. As if they were not going to take my babies, as if it were all a big dream— or a nightmare.

I just could not get over the fact that God would make this decision.

How could He after all I had been through?

I got put into the hospital on Sunday, I had a thyroid storm on Tuesday, I got out of the ICU and learned about the girls on Friday, and we left for Birmingham on Monday. Two questions kept running through my mind: Why did

God allow me to live through the storm if He was going to let my babies die?

Why would He save my life just to take it away?

CHAPTER 7

I lost all will to speak to anyone other than my husband about my feelings and my heart. I gave him my cell phone from this point on and left the calls and messages up to him. This probably wasn't fair to him, but I could not communicate with the outside world. When I spoke to people, I was grateful to hear their sympathies, but I knew they were living normal lives and I was still in the midst of my painful journey that felt never-ending and so unfair. My friends, my sister, and my church family had all had healthy pregnancies and sweet babies. How was I supposed to talk to them, look at them, and not be resentful?

We left for Birmingham soon after and met with one more maternal fetal medicine doctor specializing in TTTS. He had seen hundreds of cases, many very difficult, and was prepared to help us out. When we had the first ultrasound, I could not even look at the screen, and I requested no pictures. It was too difficult to connect with these sweet girls one more time when they wouldn't be mine much longer. The ultrasound tech seemed confused about this and I couldn't explain it other than they were not going to make it. After meeting with Dr. O, he said this was a very difficult case. One in every ten thousand pregnancies results in twin-to-twin transfusion syndrome. In TTTS, there are five stages, four being death of both babies. I was at a stage 4. In most cases, the pregnancy was farther along and the babies much bigger. The surgery is usually done on babies after twenty weeks; mine were at sixteen weeks. He also said that there are usually few connecting cords; my girls had several. These all lined up to horrible circumstances. He was also concerned about my health and making the trip for a surgery, but with all the odds against us, he still felt like we could have the surgery instead of aborting our precious girls. He knew we were sent there to terminate the pregnancy, but he didn't want that to be an option for us.

You remember how I kept questioning God's plan and didn't think it should go this way? Well, He knew better and had a plan; I just lacked the faith to see it. So we left there that Friday afternoon with hope again.

> Just as you cannot understand the path of the
> wind or the mystery of a tiny baby growing in
> its mothers womb. So you cannot understand
> the activity of God who does all things.
> —Ecclesiastes 11:5

In Corrie Ten Boom's book *The Hiding Place,* she and her sister Betsy talk about 1 Thessalonians 5:18. Her sister reminds her to give thanks in all circumstances, not just the comfortable and pleasing ones. In her book, they gave thanks for the fleas that bit them every night while lying on their molded straw mats to gain an ounce of sleep while in concentration camps. The fleas resulted in the gospel being shared and souls being saved. The fleas are what kept the guards out of the common rooms so the gospel could be shared.

In my situation, I was reluctant to give thanks also. I did not want to give thanks for what was happening, what we were being sent to do. I didn't even want to give thanks for saving my life, if losing two more would have been the outcome.

But like in her book, the most terrible petulance resulted in something much more as a result of the Lord Almighty and His unwavering love.

I love those girls with every ounce of my being, but God loves me even more than that. It is almost impossible to fathom how much love that really is.

This surgery is only conducted in three hospitals in the United States. Our best option, the most highly recommended, was in Cincinnati, Ohio.

We were to leave out that Sunday morning following our unexpected good news we received at Friday's appointment. At our church, we had an e-mail chain where prayer requests were posted. My sister-in-law had been keeping it updated with our progressing pregnancy. Within four hours, our church raised a little over $2,700 that Saturday morning. We carried the money with us, and it was spent very quickly on medical expenses and hotel stays. Once we arrived in Cincinnati, we checked in to the nearest hotel, right across from the hospital, because I had to be within five minutes in case of an emergency.

CHAPTER 8

I love the Lord, because he hath heard my voice and my supplications. Because he hath inclined his ear unto me, therefore I will call upon Him as long as I live. The sorrows of death surrounded me and the pains of hell laid hold upon me: I found trouble and sorrow.

—Psalm 116:1:3

We had the first ultrasound the next day, and my first question was "Are they both still alive?"

Yes! They were!

We were assigned an entire team of doctors, nurses, anesthesiologists, nurse practitioners, and more. Our new maternal fetal medicine doctor was from Tennessee—right down the road! God was trying to make us feel at home and comforted in such an uncomfortable situation and place. I had an MRI to show us a clear picture of the girls, and afterward we watched it on a screen the size of a wall in the conference room with our team.

I felt like I was on an episode of a TV show.

Lucas and I walked into this room and sat to the side of the huge table. We were out of our element big time! They quickly informed us that we were the reason for this team being assembled and we deserved the seats at the table.

In this conference, we realized I had six sacks in my womb. One that both girls were in and five more—all filled with amniotic fluid. My body produced this for seven babies!

They didn't form though. Whew! I would have not been ready for that! After the meeting, they concluded that they would perform the surgery to separate the cords. We signed the paperwork and agreed.

They told us that we had a 75 percent chance of survival for both babies. This gave me such a renewed sense of hope that I had been lacking for some time.

Our doctor set us up with contacts to check into the Ronald McDonald house in Cincinnati, and thankfully, out of the fifteen days, we spent twelve days there. The people we met were so encouraging and kind. We were very humbled and very blessed to have been a great part of this ministry. This is where I realized that no matter how this turned out, it could be worse. I could have a child suffering here for years, fighting battles that I, as the mother, couldn't help them win.

During the stay, we spent Thanksgiving. I really wanted some good southern home-cooked food, or as close as I could get to it, and there was nothing to be found. We thought Cracker Barrel would do, but the wait was *hours* long. We then decided we could settle for the Golden Corral. The wait was two hours. Apparently people in

Cincinnati don't cook on Thanksgiving but eat out instead! We finally, on the verge of starvation, pulled into a Mexican restaurant, which believe it or not, was also packed! Who eats Mexican food on Thanksgiving? Well, we did. When we got back to the Ronald McDonald House, volunteers had come in and cooked a huge Thanksgiving feast. How awesome is that?

I began feeling pains and started hurting very badly beneath the babies. I thought it was just gas pains, so Lucas and I searched for gas relief medicine. It was late at night and I was in pajamas and slippers and did not care at all! We went to the nearest grocery store. In the south, most chain grocery stores are usually in clean areas and you don't have to worry about your safety. But there? No.

We pulled up to a stoplight on this dark street before we found the store and a police officer came up beside us. He said, "What are you doing?" The light was red and we were law-abiding citizens, so we were stopped. He said, "You don't stop here at night. You'll get shot!" Needless to say, we ran that red light.

We entered the store and there was a sign on neon poster board that said, "No purses or bags allowed." Officers in there were arresting a man for shoplifting. I clung to Lucas's arm and held on for dear life. If I wouldn't have been hurting so bad, I would have left that place in a heartbeat. I did fit in though in my slippers and PJs!

The next day, I told my doctor about this and he conducted an ultrasound on my ovaries. He said. "Your ovaries are huge and very cystic, full of knots. They are twisting, which causes the pain. When you have a C-section and they see your ovaries, do not let them take them out because they look like they are eaten up with cancer. This is just from the pregnancy. They will return to normal." Talk about one more scare! I just left this in God's hands and focused on the girls.

My ovaries did return to normal after the pregnancy.

CHAPTER 9

Then called I upon the name of the Lord; O Lord, I beseech thee, deliver my soul. Gracious is the Lord, and righteous; yea, our God is merciful. The Lord preserves the simple: I was brought low and He helped me.

—Psalm 116:4–6

We prepared for the surgery and prayed with my father-in-law, mother-in-law, husband, and mother. I was at the hospital early that morning and became very nervous. Not for myself but for the girls. I can remember crying and saying how scared I was and looking at my father-in-law. There were tears running down his cheek, but this man's faith held me in those moments. Looking at him, I knew it would be okay. He was there and he was holding onto his faith for the both of us. His trust in the Lord covered me and gave me the peace I needed.

They took me back into an operating room of about twenty people. They put me under anesthesia and began the surgery. I woke up and told the nurse I needed some more "happy juice" to fall asleep again. She informed me they were finishing up and I could feel the tugs of little cords coming out of my stomach.

During the surgery, they took pictures of the girls with a camera that was inside my womb on a wire. We had these pictures printed and cherish them dearly. The girls had twenty-three connecting blood vessels. Even in Cincinnati, this was *extremely* rare and almost *unheard of.*

Following the surgery, I became very ill once again. I had a reaction to the anesthesia—a bad one. I had never been that sick in my life and hope to never be again. My husband even became very ill, either from sympathy pains or from the White Castle cheeseburger in the hospital vending machine. He left to take a shower and rest back at the Ronald McDonald House.

> Return unto thy rest, O my soul; for the Lord
> hath dealt bountifully with thee. For thou
> has delivered my soul from death, mine eyes
> from tears, and my feet from falling.
> —Psalm 116:7

When he was gone, November 24, 2012, the following day, I was alone in the hospital room when a very tall, middle-aged doctor came in. I will never forget those next few minutes.

He sat down to complete a follow-up ultrasound beside my hospital bed. He didn't say much, but he put his hand on my bed and gently said, "Baby B did not make it. I am so sorry, but there is no heartbeat." He further explained that Ainsley Pearl ultimately sacrificed herself, her blood, for Lilly Grace. There could only be one.

I don't know where the strength came from, but in kind, I responded, "It's okay. I was prepared for this. I knew it might be coming."

I still do not know where those words came from, or how on earth I did not break down in tears.

After he left, I called Lucas and told him she didn't have a heart beat, and he knew it was Ainsley Pearl. I cried sharing this on the phone with him, and that was the last time I shed a tear until the day Lilly Grace was born.

I chose to trust God. If I were to rely on my emotions rather than my faith, I do not know how I would have been able to pull through that moment. I did not feel God was there in that cold hospital room with me like I had felt his presence before, but in my heart, underneath the layers of brokenness, I knew He was. And He wouldn't leave me.

As it says in Romans 8:35 and 38–39,

Who shall separate us from the love of Christ? Shall tribulation, or distress, or persecution, or famine, or nakedness, or peril, or sword? For I am persuaded, that neither death, nor life, nor angels, nor powers, nor things

present, nor things to come, not height, nor depth, nor
any other creature, shall be able to separate us from
the love of God, which is in Christ Jesus our Lord.

Not my near death, my daughter's death, any powers
of the devil, any medicine, or anything that is yet to come
can separate me from the love of God.

We may not always feel the love or be convinced of
the love when we are struggling, but it's still there. It's
unconditional, even when we want to give up. His love
doesn't leave—ever.

I called upon the Lord in distress: the Lord answered
me, and set me in a large place. The Lord is on my
side, I will not fear: what can man do to me?

—Psalm 118:5–6

Chapter 10

Just days after this, we named the girls. This was difficult for me. We met with counselors presurgery and they asked if we had named the girls. I responded, "Not yet. I don't want to name them until we know they will be okay." In hindsight, I wish I had. We decided on Ainsley Pearl after my husband's great grandmother Pearl's fighting spirit. And we decided on Lilly Grace—Lilly after my husband's aunt who died from ovarian cancer and Grace because it would only be by the grace of God if she made it into this world.

I felt like I built a wall up to shield myself from the pain during this time. Looking back, I feel like God knew I was at my limit and my emotions needed a break. He took my torment, fear, pain, anxiety, and anger and absorbed them so that I didn't have to deal with it at that time. The thing was I had to be strong. And I had to carry Lilly Grace alive, and Ainsley Pearl's body only, in my womb until delivery.

After coming home, I was on bed rest once again, but this time in a wheelchair for a few weeks recovering. I had checkups weekly with my regular OB and my OB in Birmingham. My AFI, amniotic fluid, began to look low, and I had to receive IV fluids once again, along with drinking massive amounts of water, which I did not like in the least. The OB did not want to take any chances with her. During my surgery, the doctors took five pounds of amniotic fluid off me, simply because I did not need it. It was crowding the girls. This was fine at the time, but it caused me to leak fluid from the incision into the womb. During a stay for more fluids, my water broke and I was to remain in the hospital to prevent infection.

I felt like a water fountain with IV fluids going in and—well, you get the picture. Needless to say, I was in adult diapers!

I felt pain one night in the hospital and began to have some complications. I thought I was going into labor, but it was a false alarm. I hurt for the next two weeks with my water broken and being on constant IV fluids and antibiotics until I finally went into actual labor on March 12, 2013, two months before my due date. Lilly-Grace was finally coming into this world.

They began me on more medicine to progress the labor and dilate me further. I received my epidural, which hit a vein and caused a great deal of pain. Then they tried again for a second time, hitting it spot on.

I labored for twelve hours but only pushed for eighteen minutes. This was actually the easiest part of the pregnancy. Since things were in a stable state, they allowed me to birth Lilly-Grace, which I am very thankful for. We did not know until she was born whether or not she would have cerebral palsy. So we waited, knowing we would love her all the same.

When she was born, she weighed four pounds and one ounce and was sixteen inches long. She was delivered first, and her daddy got to see her before I did. They wrapped her up, let me look at her, and whisked her away to the neonatal ICU. They then delivered Ainsley Pearl along with most of my placenta. The doctor who performed the delivery was not my actual doctor but the on-call OB, so she did not really know my entire situation.

Ainsely Pearl was so small that she was inside my placenta. Lucas and I both discussed if we wanted to see her, but the OB knew that we should probably keep our memories of her the way she was, rather than the state her body was in that day. We made the choice not to look. Her soul was already with Jesus. He was holding her hand and cradling her in His arms in heaven, just like I would get to with her sister here on earth. Some people may ask how I was so accepting of this, how I was not mad or more upset. This would come later, but in these moments, I just had the peace of God that passed all understanding. It didn't leave me but helped me continue on.

I remember people saying months after, "You're so strong. You're so strong." I would say, "I'm not," because I didn't feel that I really was. If that pregnancy were up to me, I would have crumpled like a wet tissue.

I am not strong, The great I AM is strong,

And he was living in me and through me.

Chapter 11

I t was challenging for me to deal with my emotions. I was happy, as a new mother should be, at the birth of my baby girl, but also sad at the death of my other. I shoved my emotions back into a jar in the back of my mind and put a lid on it until I could deal with them.

I began to focus more and more on Lilly-Grace. I spent every hour that was allowed in the NICU with her. I took myself off all pain medication so I could drive myself back and forth while she was there. Even when I couldn't hold her, I just watched her through the glass and we stared at each other. She was healthy—no disabilities at all! Those are some very sweet memories that I will always hold dear to my heart.

Lilly-Grace did wonderfully. She got moved to a crib and had her feeding tube removed all in the same day. We came to see her bright and early Sunday morning, and they surprised us with the news she could come home! We had been praying about this since her birth, and you know what? *It was also Easter.* The day the Lord rose again and saw His mother, Mary, he allowed our little miracle to come home with her mommy and daddy.

We have cherished Lilly Grace like no other. She is such a joy and a light in our lives and a blessing beyond any other. She is a miracle, and we make sure she knows all about her Father, the Lord Jesus Christ. Without him, she would not be here, and neither would I. Often in life, we take so many things for granted.

This experience changed my life. It brought me closer to the Lord than I ever thought possible. It taught me to appreciate what we have been given, to not let the little things pass us by. To not hold on to money, possessions, or things in this world but to hold on to the ones we love and, most importantly, to our faith in the Lord.

I'm not saying things have always been easy; they have not. We have had some scares with Lilly-Grace and faced much sickness because of her low immune system, but look at the grace the Lord has given us.

I am still in awe, and I always will be.

In the statistics of TTTS survival children, all but 5 percent have learning delays, and most develop leukocytes on their brain, which cause disabilities such as autism. But since Lilly-Grace has been two years old, she has shown more progression in her academic development than children twice her age. My husband likes to think that the Lord gave Lilly Grace Ainsley Pearl's wit and personality as well!

After bringing Lilly-Grace home, it began to sink in more and more that she was the only one. It seemed as if I were in some sort of alternative reality where things weren't real. At times, I would just sit and think, *I can't believe this.* Often, in the dark of the night, after Lilly-Grace had gone to bed, I would lay in Lucas's arms and cry. If I ever let the guard down, I felt like drowning in my own grief. I kept the wall up most of the time, never letting myself think too much about her. When I did, it became too much to bear. I would live in a bubble and block out the grief and torture my mind and body went through.

When out grocery shopping, I saw a set of twins and can remember feeling so much resentment and pain at that moment. It wasn't right, and it wasn't fair, but it was real.

When Lilly Grace began to speak well at around two years old, she pointed to a ring of light on the ceiling that was reflecting off a candle. She said, "Look, Mommy. It's Jesus." She continued telling me this over and over, and I couldn't understand where she was referring to. I picked her up and she pointed directly at the ring of light on the ceiling. She said, "That's Jesus." She didn't know that light represented Jesus or that the halo, a ring of light, was the symbol worn on the heads of angels. Just the next day, I was doing laundry and came into the living room hearing her talk. She was carrying on the cutest conversation, and I said to her, "Baby, who are you talking to?" She replied, "My sister."

This was before we had told her anything about her sister.

God works in mysterious ways, and his presence is all around us. Sometimes it takes the most innocent to recognize it.

We have made Ainsley Pearl a big part of our life. When Lilly Grace began to understand, we told her all about her sister in heaven. She loved looking at her pictures and tells many people about her. She is someone who should be celebrated and remembered. When I think of her now, I know she would look just like Lilly Grace, and I picture her and Jesus holding hands walking around heaven. I think of Him telling her stories about the animals on the ark, how He fed the hungry and healed the sick, and she is smiling up at Him while sitting on his knee. Love and happiness beam from her, and she never feels the pain she would have felt here on the earth. Her kidneys are healthy. She's strong and beautiful and precious.

CHAPTER 12

Last year, Cincinnati called me and asked to conduct a study on Lilly-Grace. I gave them all of her medical records and mine as well. We scheduled the trip, and two weeks before it was time to leave, I broke down.

The lid finally came off that jar I mentioned earlier.

Over the next several months, I faced depression, anxiety, and doubt. I had never feared so much. I was afraid that the Lord might do something to Lilly Grace or to me, to get my attention and to pull me back closer to him.

I was angry with God for taking Ainsley Pearl, and I wanted to know why. I felt resentment. Was I not good enough? Did He not think I could raise twins? I fought through many tough questions and felt I had lost my intimate relationship with God.

I prayed that the Lord would lead me to someone and started to search for Christian counselors in our area. The first person I found was within forty-five miles of me. I called and left a message right away. I began to see her within the week, and she and I worked through many of my issues.

On my drive back and forth in the beginning, I can remember I would call out to God and yell, "Why? Why?"

I was finally allowing myself to feel angry and feel the buried emotions that I had so strongly rejected earlier in my journey.

I learned a lot there, most importantly that God did not hurt me; He healed me. God did not punish me; He redeemed me. God did not save me to put me through so much heartache and pain; He rescued me from the sinking ship. In this world, we will face tribulation, not as a result of our wrongdoings but as a result of Adam's sin.

As Angie Smith states in her book *I Will Carry You.*

He isn't threatened by a rainstorm, He knows that rain will fall. He knows that I will fall. I gave my deepest hurt to the Father who wanted nothing less than every bit of it. What I needed to learn about myself was clear in that moment. I did believe in Him enough to call out. I trusted Him enough to share the brokenness, even though He already knew it all. I thought about what it must feel like not only to know that one of your children is hurting but what it would mean to you if she told you herself- if she came to you because she wanted it to be a shared grief. And so, I let him into a place I had never fully invited Him before. A place of communion where I could rest knowing He heard me.

Sometimes fear will try to creep back into my mind, but I know that, according to 2 Timothy 1:7, "God has not given us the spirit of fear; but of power, and of love, and of a sound mind."

I learned that this world is hard, it will always be hard, and bad things will continue to happen, but when the bridge breaks and the raging waters start rushing in, the Lord is there, in the water with you, holding you over His head so that He suffers before you. That's it. That's the key. He has already done it. He suffered for me, and for you, and for us all.

I know that my testimony was given to me to share with others, to try to help someone else who may be struggling out there in this tough world. "We know that all things work together for good to them that love God, to them who are called according to His purpose" (Romans 8:28).

The unseen hand is always with us, open and ready for us to grab on and never let go.

CHAPTER 13

Following the birth of Lilly-Grace and the sweet homecoming, the bills began to pour in like rain. We had already spent $10,000 of our money saved up on these bills and had little to none left for the year. Bills from Birmingham, University Hospital in Cincinnati, Children's Hospital in Cincinnati, and Huntsville Hospital began to pile up quickly.

We paid each month like we were supposed to, but the collectors wanted more. I explained our situation to them again and again with different agents, but they didn't care.

They threatened to turn us over to collection agencies, but this was all we could do.

Our close friends and family decided to put on a benefit for us, to help with the overwhelming amounts of bills we owed, which at this point was around $43,000 after insurance. The benefit came together quickly and miraculously. The outpouring of love and generosity from our community was amazing! By the end of the night, the benefit had raised $25,000. We could not be more blessed! We paid off Birmingham and both hospitals in Cincinnati and then arranged a meeting to pay off Huntsville. After arriving at the billing office, I asked our account manager if we could get a discount for paying the bill off in cash. I laid the cash on the desk, and she said exclaimed, "Oh my, I didn't think you meant literal cash!" It probably looked like a drug deal, and I'm sure I shocked the woman.

I explained about the benefit our community held, and she stopped me halfway through. I had never met this woman before in my life. She said, "You're the woman with the twins." I said, "Yes, I had twins." And she said Ainsley

Pearl's name. I wanted to cry right there in that office. She knew me! She had heard about my benefit and donated pies to auction off! She settled my account with me, and after leaving that office, we had paid off all hospital debts and gotten back our $10,000 to live on for the remainder of the year. God was in every single aspect of this! He was taking care of us! We never went without; even when we thought we had no more, the Lord always came through.

In sharing our grief, a wise Christian man, recently told us, "I often questioned God during my times of grief, but then I realized that I got the chance to love my child." He said I should listen to "The Dance" by Garth Brooks. I took his advice and this simple country song took on a new depth for me.

Our lives are better left to chance, I could have missed the pain, but I'd have had to miss the dance.

If I could change the hardships—the grief, the pain, or any of it—I wouldn't. My life is left to God. It's all in His plan, and like the song says, if I missed the pain, I would have missed the dance of loving my child—both of them. Ainsley Pearl may have not had a long life, but she had the most love a child could possible receive while she was here. And we got the gift of loving her. That was God's gift to us, the opportunity to love her just a little while before He loved on her forever.

As I have continued to share my story, I feel the love of women all around me who have struggles with similar things. You would not believe the number of women who have faced loss.

As I was talking with a mother recently while visiting the Ronald McDonald House in Birmingham, I realized that we shared so much in common, even though we had never met. We had different jobs, hobbies, friends, families, and churches, and we looked different as well, but in talking with this inspiring woman, I realized we shared a much deeper bond. We were the mothers of life— and of loss.

While we were talking, we shared our testimonies with each other as if we were longtime friends. She shared how her daughter was stillborn with no warning, and I told her about Ainsley Pearl. We talked about the stages of grief but how we have used it to guide us more toward God. We also talked about how mothers really feel—how we question ourselves and our bodies and how we need to place blame somewhere in order to survive the guilt we put on ourselves as mothers. We also talked about how the easiest and most common target to place this ugly blame is on God, when He is the last one to deserve it. Thank the Lord that the blame game doesn't last long and that the Lord is forgiving.

Acceptance is the worst phase of the grief and the most challenging, in my opinion. Many women never get there and the grief becomes their identity. This is not what the Lord wants. According to Jeremiah 29:11, the Lord know the plans He has for us and they are for our *good,* not for us to dwell on the loss but to allow good to come from our sufferings.

CHAPTER 14

O ne year later, Lilly-Grace was being dedicated to the Lord at our church. This was a very simple ceremony where all the parents in the church dedicated to raise their children in the ways of the Lord and to commit to teaching their children as the Bible tells us to. I was kind of overseeing this process and handing out the little pink and blue Bibles. I think that this was to keep my mind busy. I tend to keep busy to occupy my mind, and this was at a time that was especially difficult for me.

When holidays and major events happen, I often think back to my precious baby girl in heaven, thinking there should be two here; I should be doing this with two girls. It always makes it more difficult for me knowing exactly what she would look like, seeing that they were both identical twins. I know what she was as a baby, but wishing I could have seen her growing up and knowing that she would have looked just like Lilly-Grace makes it easy for my mind to envision her there too. It almost makes it more difficult for me to grieve because I seem to have to do it again and again at different stages in Lilly-Grace's life. Of course I celebrate her life, but I also see her without a missing piece of herself and of our family.

I made it through the service without crying, but as I walked outside, I lost it. There, in the sky, right in front of the church, was a set of double rainbows. I knew in that instant that she was there.

Identical, beautiful twin rainbows were a sign for me to know that I had one here, dedicating her to the Lord, and the other in heaven with the Lord, already dedicated to him. In heart, they were still side by side, in the Lord's hands forever. This is not the only time that the Lord had shown me this sign. I never see it when things are going well, only when I am stressed and dealing with difficult moments. The double rainbows appear, I feel, as a sign to me from the Lord, my God, that He is still there and always will be.

I was shopping in a thrift store in Alabama, and my aunt was with me, as was Lilly-Grace. We found this picture in a frame that melted my heart. If you can picture this, there were two girls, identical twins, looking at each other. They were both holding puppies. The amazing thing was that one was an angel and one was not. I immediately thought of the girls when I saw this. The twins in the picture had blue eyes and blond, curly hair, just like my girls. I bought it, of course, and hung it in her room.

This again was a sign from God, I feel. This is when things hit me hard. As I looked at those little girls in that picture later that night and in the coming days, I couldn't help but think of her as a toddler. Before, I had her picture with me as a baby. I knew what she looked like and her sweet face, but in this frame, I could see the curly, blonde hair and the sweet, blue eyes. I thought of her then not as a baby but as a little girl. I thought of what I missed, or was going to miss, including how I wouldn't get to brush her hair and tell her stories and bedtime. I thought of how we wouldn't get to color together and talk about boys. I thought about how I wouldn't get to take pictures of her in her prom dress and embarrass her with scrapbook pictures of when she was little. I thought about how I wouldn't get to help her get into her gown on her wedding day and how I wouldn't be there at the birth of her children. How I wouldn't get the phone calls in the middle of the night about how hard motherhood was. I would miss her whole life. Her sister would miss her best friend. Twins were supposed to be best friends forever, and she would miss it too. It didn't seem real; it didn't seem manageable.

I was reading this book to Lilly-Grace one day, and it spoke of heaven and what it would be like there. In the book were pictures of toddlers playing in heaven, and it looked like so much fun! It spoke of the hurts being healed and the perfect and new bodies we would have. It gave me such joy and peace, this children's book, to get a visual image in my mind of how she was living much more fully in heaven than she would have been down here on earth.

The day before I was giving my testimony for the first time, I took Lilly-Grace to the pumpkin patch with a friend of hers. Her mom and I were talking about my pregnancy and hers while the girls played on the slides.

She did not know our daughter's name, Ainsley Pearl. She said, "Oh, I know a little girl named that!"

My gut reaction was "What?"

It seemed unreal and unfair at first. I always knew there had to be someone else named Ainsley out there, but both of the names?

Later that night, my mom, Lilly-Grace, and I went on an outing to Goodwill, and I texted my friend to hear once more that I hadn't just imagined what she'd told me. She said, "Yes, the little girl's name is Ainsley Pearl, and she goes to the same nursery care as my daughter. Her name is spelled the same way too."

I started to tear up right in between the coats and sweaters aisle. I told her how crazy this all was, and she then informed me that the little girl was named after her daddy's grandmother.

Okay, at first, I was thinking, *Is this a slap in the face from the devil the night before I give my testimony, trying to bring me down before I tell about the power of God?*

But then, as she told me that, I knew the devil has no power like the Lord. Our Ainsley Pearl was also named after her daddy's grandmother Pearl. The more we talked, the more I realized God was there, and I felt like it was His way of letting Ainsley Pearl tell me it was okay to tell people about her the next night. I went into the Good Will dressing room and got on my knees—yes, on the floor! And I praised the Lord. I just cried and repeatedly said, "Thank you, Lord. I praise your name. I love you, God." I probably said it thirty times and couldn't think of anything else.

The next day, I was nervous before I was to give my testimony at 6:00 that night. At 3:30, I got down on my knees to pray in the living room floor, and as I bowed my head, right there in front of me were two rainbows shining through the glass window onto the carpet. I laid my hands on each of them and again just began to pray to the Lord. I asked forgiveness for doubting Him and continually thanked the Lord over and over again for His presence in my life. I thanked Him for healing that hurt and for the wisdom to see that my heavenly Father was with me. I told Him how much I loved Him and how thankful I was to Him for giving me this gift that to some may seem small but to me was so incredibly huge!

Epilogue: Letter to Ainsley Pearl

Hello, my sweet girl,

Today is the day you went to heaven four years ago. Sorry it has taken me so long to write, but you see, even though you're happy there, it is still hard for me here on earth without you. It was hard for Mommy to write to you, but you know what? God told me to. I know that you and Jesus are really close and He protects you up there. He doesn't let you feel hurt, and since you got to go to heaven early, you have never known what hurt feels like. I am so thankful for that! And guess what. Today is Thanksgiving! That is what I am most thankful for: for you and Lilly-Grace and Daddy, but most of all for Jesus. If we didn't have Him, there would be no one to keep you safe. I am also thankful that the Lord saved my life so that I could trust him with my little girl. I pray for your sister that she will also be saved at a young age so that she will never have to know what it feels like to be without Jesus.

Today, we went to the back of the farm and let a dozen white balloons go into the sky. Lilly-Grace wanted to do this so that you could have them in heaven. We watched them float up and up until we couldn't see them anymore. She said that you had them now and that you and Molly would play with them. Molly used to chase balloons and try and pop them with her mouth. I hope you love them.

Everyone here misses you all the time, but that's just us being selfish because we know that you're so happy up there. What does your room look like? Lilly-Grace wants to know your favorite color; she says it's probably pink like hers. Is there a swimming pool? The other day, the moon had clouds over it and your sister said that you probably colored on it with a permanent marker. Can you see the moon from heaven?

Today is hard. I have really not enjoyed this holiday since we lost you. I don't like thinking about that time in Cincinnati, Ohio. I don't like going back there in my mind, and at this time of year, it's hard for me not to do that. This year has been better though. I have tried to focus on what I am thankful for.

We didn't go to Thanksgiving this year; I just wanted to spend time at home. Some people in the family didn't quite understand and thought we should be around people to take our minds off things, but that's really the last thing I wanted to do. We are distracted the other days of the year. I wanted to spend this day, your day, remembering you and celebrating you.

I know that you have seen me cry a lot over the past four years, but I don't want you to think I am upset with you at all. I just cry sometimes because I miss you and I wish you were here. Lilly-Grace has been saying a lot lately that she wishes you were here. All I can say is, "I know. Me too."

I want you to know that you gave me the best gift. You gave me courage. A story to tell. A testimony. You have given me the will to speak and tell others about you. I feel like the best way for me to celebrate your life is to share it with others. Since I have told people about you, many other women have shared with me too. I don't know God's plan for me yet, but I know he wants me to keep telling people about you. I tell you I love you all the time. I hope you can hear me. Just know that Mommy does love you so so so much. We all do, baby girl. We love you as far as the east is from the west, and nothing could ever take that away.

You are our angel, and we will always miss you.